The
LOVER'S
QUOTATION
BOOK

The

LOVER'S
QUOTATION
BOOK

A Literary Companion

BARNES
&NOBLE
BOOKS
NEW YORK

2000 Barnes & Noble Books

ISBN 0-7607-1685-4

00 01 02 03 04 MC 9 8 7 6 5 4 3 2 1

FG

PREFACE

Who's equal to uttering the last word on love? From Ovid to Chaucer, Shakespeare to Colette, many have tried to find le mot juste, to hold in language the elusive, fluctuating quality of romantic love. And in the effort, surprising discoveries have been made. The well-turned phrase seems to be one step ahead of us, and wiser. Love heals, and it wounds. And out of the wounds, some of the best— and funniest— writing comes. We're all poets in the province of love. Moreover, descriptions about love in phrases that are often beautiful and agile, feats of the imagination that can dazzle and amaze, awaken recognition within each of us.

In reading through these quotations, one thing becomes clear: the paramount, immediate pleasure men and women continually speak of is the pleasure of loving and being loved; and they voice this conviction with a confidence in the vitality of love which remains alive regardless of its surroundings. No love, writers tell us, is equal to another; each must be enshrined in unique phrases. Some are personal, others universal; some are decorated with images and fanciful grace notes; others are witty and ironic or perplexed and bewildered. Many were uttered in an effort to distinguish unforgettably that indefinable quality or blessing that transforms life and perhaps to have the effect of making that sensation and that experience last forever.

Long or short, the quotations bear witness to a faith in the inner life which gives cohesion to the changing, outward pageant. No reader can fail to appreciate the efforts of so many people to define this indispensible portion of our existence. And no anthologist can hope to bring all of the fascinating and varied statements together between the covers of one volume. The Lover's Quotation Book is merely one effort to extract from several writers in order to compose an eclectic picture of love, and it is an invitation to the reader to hear in the voices the passing and changing echo of particular moments in his or her own life.

To the quotations here, I urge readers to add their own. You may surprise yourself, as I did, and find new ideas springing into mind. And you'll surely rediscover the magical persuasion of language: the mere act of saying makes things happen.

With many thanks to Bill Henderson, whose unerring instinct for a happy idea gave shape to these pages; and my appreciation to William Cole, whose edition of W.H. Auden's Commonplace Book *started my own collection.*

HELEN HANDLEY
New York City

The
LOVER'S
QUOTATION
BOOK

And the Lord God caused a deep sleep to fall upon Adam, and he slept: and he took one of his ribs and closed up the flesh instead thereof; and the rib, which the Lord God had taken from man, made he a woman, and brought her unto the man. And Adam said, This is now bone of my bones, and flesh of my flesh: she shall be called Woman, because she was taken out of Man. Therefore shall a man leave his father and mother, and shall cleave unto his wife: and they shall be one flesh.

GENESIS

What happiness to be beloved; and O,
What bliss, ye gods, to love!

JOHANN WOLFGANG GOETHE

Any time that is not spent on love is wasted.

TASSO

Love is a constant interrogation. In fact, I don't know of a better definition of love.

MILAN KUNDERA

Falling In Love is a phenomenon of attention, but of an abnormal state of attention which occurs in a normal man.

ORTEGA Y GASSET

The great tragedy of life is not that men perish, but that they cease to love.

W. SOMERSET MAUGHAM

In love there is always one who kisses and one who offers the cheek.

FRENCH PROVERB

Money cannot buy love, but it makes shopping for it a lot easier.

ANONYMOUS

Love which is all-inclusive seems to repel us.

HENRY MILLER

Love is like an hourglass, with the heart filling up as the brain empties.

JULES RENARD

Compared to other feelings, love is an elemental cosmic force wearing a disguise of meekness. In itself it is as simple and unconditional as consciousness and as death, as oxygen or uranium. It is not a state of mind, it is the foundation of the universe.

BORIS PASTERNAK

An ideal of love: To love with all desire and yet to be as kind as an old man past desire.

W.B. YEATS

I have a stinking hangover and don't speak on the ride back, don't even think much except to tell myself how much jabber there is in the name of love.

LILLIAN HELLMAN

(though love be a day and life be nothing, it shall not stop kissing).

E.E. CUMMINGS

When you fall in love with someone, you're finished. It's always like that!

FRANCOISE SAGAN

Love is the triumph of imagination over intelligence.

H.L. MENCKEN

Love has as few problems as a motor car. The only problems are the driver, the passengers, and the road.

FRANZ KAFKA

The love that lasts the longest is the love that is never returned.

W. SOMERSET MAUGHAM

Love is a springtime plant that perfumes everything with its hope, even the ruins to which it clings.

GUSTAVE FLAUBERT

Where love rules, there is no will to power; and where power predominates, there love is lacking. The one is the shadow of the other.

C.G. JUNG

Love is like a superb disease, shameful when it isn't shared.

FRANCOISE SAGAN

Those whom we can love, we can hate; to others we are indifferent.

HENRY DAVID THOREAU

As soon as you cannot keep anything from a woman, you love her.

PAUL GERALDY

'Tis better to have loved and lost,
Than never to have loved at all.

ALFRED, LORD TENNYSON

Love is a smoke raised with the fume of sighs,
Being purged, a fire sparkling in lover's eyes,
Being vexed, a sea nourished with lover's tears.
What is it else? A madness, most discreet,
A choking gall, and a preservëd sweet.

WILLIAM SHAKESPEARE

All the things of my life I loved and kept on loving through parting, and not through meeting, through pulling away, and not through coming together, not unto life but unto death.

MARINA TSVETAEVA

If no love is, O God, what fele I so?
And if love is, what thing and which is he?
If love be good, from whennes cometh my woo?

GEOFFREY CHAUCER

Love itself is the most elitist of passions. It acquires its stereoscopic substance and perspective only in the context of culture, for it takes up more place in the mind than it does in the bed. Outside of that setting it falls flat into one-dimensional fiction.

JOSEPH BRODSKY

Love is an egotism of two.

ANTOINE DE LA SALE

Love is a naked child: do you think he has pockets for money?

OVID

Love . . . is a projection of that maternal or paternal cannibalism which desires to hug what belongs to it, even unto death.

J.C. POWYS

Love, with very young people, is a heartless business. We drink at that age from thirst, or to get drunk; it is only later in life that we occupy ourselves with the individuality of our wine.

ISAK DINESEN

Love is either the shrinking remnant of something which was once enormous; or else it is part of something which will grow in the future into something enormous. But in the present it does not satisfy. It gives much less than one expects.

ANTON CHEKHOV

What I say is that the supreme and singular joy of making love resides in the certainty of doing evil.
CHARLES BAUDELAIRE

The crowded terror that is human love.
YVOR WINTERS

It is love, and not German philosophy, that is the true explanation of this world, whatever may be the explanation of the next.
OSCAR WILDE

People who are sensible about love are incapable of it.
DOUGLAS YATES

In love and war don't seek counsel.
FRENCH PROVERB

True love is like seeing ghosts: we all talk about it, but few of us have ever seen one.
LA ROCHEFOUCAULD

Love, in distinction from friendship, is killed, or rather extinguished, the moment it is displayed in public.
HANNAH ARENDT

Love is a spaniel that prefers even punishment from one hand to caresses from another.
CHARLES CALEB COLTON

Love demands all, and has a right to it.
BEETHOVEN

Love and eggs are best when they are fresh.
RUSSIAN PROVERB

Try to reason about love and you will lose your reason.
FRENCH PROVERB

There's more to love than love, when it's right.
JOHN O'HARA

Love is not primarily a relationship to a specific person; it is an attitude, an ordination of character which determines the relatedness of the person to the world as a whole, not towards one object of love. If a person loves only one other person and is indifferent to the rest of his fellow men, his love is not love but a symbiotic attachment, or an enlarged egotism.
ERICH FROMM

Love is a hole in the heart.
BEN HECHT

When I come back I will bring you to a plumber and let him put a ring which will enchain your leg to mine.
ENRICO CARUSO

The greatest miracle of love is that it cures one of coquetry.
LA ROCHEFOUCAULD

Human nature is so constructed that it gives affection most readily to those who seem least to demand it.

BERTRAND RUSSELL

Perfect love sometimes does not come till the first grandchild.

WELSH PROVERB

The most terrible thing of all is happy love, for then there is fear in everything.

COSIMA WAGNER

One of the deep secrets of life is that all that is really worth the doing is what we do for others.

LEWIS CARROLL

The skillful audacity required to share an inner life.

GERTRUDE STEIN

Love begins with love; friendship, however warm, cannot change to love, however mild.

LA BRUYÈRE

When love grows diseased, the best thing we can do is to put it to a violent death; I cannot endure the torture, of a lingering and consumptive passion.

GEORGE ETHEREGE

Love is blind.

GEOFFREY CHAUCER

Love's like the measles—all the worse when it comes late in life.

DOUGLAS JERROLD

Perfect love means to love the one through whom one became unhappy.

SØREN KIERKEGAARD

An old man in love is like a flower in winter.

PORTUGUESE PROVERB

There are situations, moments in life, in which, unaware, the human being confesses great portions of his ultimate personality, of his true nature. One of these situations is love. In their choice of lovers both the male and the female reveal their essential nature. The type of human being which we prefer reveals the contours of our heart.

ORTEGA Y GASSET

To love is good, too: love being difficult. For one human being to love another: that is perhaps the most difficult of all our tasks, the ultimate, the last test and proof, the work for which all other work is but preparation.

RAINER MARIA RILKE

The great secret of morals is love; or a going out of our own nature, and an identification of ourselves with the beautiful which exists in thought, action, or person, not our own.

PERCY BYSSHE SHELLEY

There is a comfort in the strength of love;
'Twill make a thing endurable, which else
Would overset the brain, or break the heart.
　　WILLIAM WORDSWORTH

Nuptial love maketh mankind, friendly love perfecteth it,
but wanton love corrupteth and embaseth it.
　　FRANCIS BACON

Friendship is a disinterested commerce between equals;
love, an abject intercourse between tyrants and slaves.
　　OLIVER GOLDSMITH

Whom we love best, to them we can say least.
　　ENGLISH PROVERB

Love is not love until love's vulnerable.
　　THEODORE ROETHKE

Some people would never have been in love, had they
never heard love talked about.
　　LA ROCHEFOUCAULD

In no love story I have ever read is a character ever *tired*. I
had to wait for Blanchot for someone to tell me about
Fatigue.
　　ROLAND BARTHES

As we all know, too much of any divine thing is destruction.

D.H. LAWRENCE

United souls are not satisfied with embraces, but desire to be truly each other; which being impossible, their desires are infinite, and proceed without a possibility of satisfaction.

SIR THOMAS BROWNE

"Faith" in the language of heaven is "Love" in the language of men.

VICTOR HUGO

Were it not for imagination, sir, a man would be as happy in the arms of a chambermaid as of a duchess.

DR. SAMUEL JOHNSON

In the mind of the kiss occurs a thought so rich
That it exonerates the astonished philosophers.

HAYDEN CARRUTH

And in fact artistic experience lies so incredibly close to that of sex, to its pain and its ecstasy, that the two manifestations are indeed but different forms of one and the same yearning delight.

RAINER MARIA RILKE

Man is in love and loves what vanishes.

W.B. YEATS

Love is, then, not a fact in nature of which we become aware, but rather a creation of the human imagination.

JOSEPH WOOD KRUTCH

I believe that the human imagination never invented anything that was not true, in this world or any other.

GERARD DE NERVAL

Love is the selfishness of two persons.

ANTOINE DE LA SALE

Love is monotonous, incessant, boring; no one would stand for anyone's repeating the most ingenious statement so many times and yet the lover demands unending reiteration that his beloved loves him. And vice versa: when someone is not in love, love bestowed upon him oppresses him and drives him mad by its utter plodding quality.

ORTEGA Y GASSET

If there is such a thing as Platonic love between a man and a woman, it is the result of some profound misunderstanding, a stifling of their true and authentic impulses.

IVAN MESTROVIC

It would be impossible to love anyone or anything one knew completely. Love is directed toward what lies hidden in its object.

PAUL VALÉRY

Take away leisure and Cupid's bow is broken.

OVID

In expressing love we belong among the undeveloped countries.

SAUL BELLOW

Why is it better to love than be loved? It is surer.

SACHA GUITRY

Don't threaten me with love, baby. Let's just go walking in the rain.

BILLIE HOLIDAY

Only little boys and old men sneer at love.

LOUIS AUCHINCLOSS

Love is not the dying moan of a distant violin—it's the triumphant twang of a bedspring.

S.J. PERELMAN

We have grown used to a Godless universe, but we are not yet accustomed to one which is loveless as well, and only when we have so become shall we realize what atheism really means.

JOSEPH WOOD KRUTCH

It is a mistake to speak of a bad choice in love, since, as soon as a choice exists, it can only be bad.

MARCEL PROUST

You are walking around
Trying to remember
What you promised
But you can't remember.

A WOMAN'S SONG (*Ojibway*)

Set me as a seal upon thine heart, as a seal upon thine arm;
for love is strong as death; jealousy is cruel as the grave; the
coals thereof are coals of fire, which hath a most vehement
flame. Many waters cannot quench love, neither can the
floods drown it.

SOLOMON'S SONG

Oh, life is a glorious cycle of song,
A medley of extemporanea;
And love is a thing that can never go wrong;
And I am Marie of Roumania.

DOROTHY PARKER

Anxiety is love's greatest killer. It makes others feel as you
might when a drowning man holds on to you. You want to
save him, but you know he will strangle you with his panic.

ANAÏS NIN

The heart is a fountain of weeping water which makes no
noise in the world.

EDWARD DAHLBERG

Love without attachment is light.

NORMAN O. BROWN

Love is the word used to label the sexual excitement of the young, the habitation of the middle-aged, and the mutual dependence of the old.

JOHN CIARDI

Love is a grave mental disease.

PLATO

When poverty comes in at doors, love leaps out at windows.

JOHN CLARKE

The only abnormality is the incapacity to love.

ANAÏS NIN

To an ordinary human being love means nothing if it does not mean loving some people more than others.

GEORGE ORWELL

Is there any stab as deep as wondering where and how you failed those you loved?

FLORIDA SCOTT-MAXWELL

Love is what you've been through with somebody.

JAMES THURBER

The word love has by no means the same sense for both sexes, and this is one cause of the serious misunderstandings that divide them.

SIMONE DE BEAUVOIR

Everybody winds up kissing the wrong person goodnight.
ANDY WARHOL

Of all the icy blasts that blow on love, a request for money is the most chilling and havoc-wreaking.
GUSTAVE FLAUBERT

All happiness or unhappiness solely depends upon the quality of the object to which we are attached by love.
SPINOZA

I don't want to live. I want to love first, and live incidentally.
ZELDA FITZGERALD

How bold one gets when one is sure of being loved.
FREUD

If one wished to be perfectly sincere, one would have to admit there are two kinds of love—well-fed and ill-fed. The rest is pure fiction.
COLETTE

There are the moments when something new has entered into us, a something unknown; our feelings grow mute in shy perplexity, everything in us withdraws, a stillness comes, and the new, which no one knows, stands in the midst of it and is silent.
RAINER MARIA RILKE

The man who is in love for the first time, even if his love is unrequited, is a godlike being.
HEINRICH HEINE

The magic of first love is our ignorance that it can ever end.
BENJAMIN DISRAELI

First love is only a little foolishness and a lot of curiosity.
BERNARD SHAW

A man content to go to heaven alone will never go to heaven.
BOETHIUS

I am not faithful but I am attached.
GÜNTER GRASS

Macho does not prove mucho.
ZSA ZSA GABOR

It takes patience to appreciate domestic bliss; volatile spirits prefer unhappiness.
GEORGE SANTAYANA

Like everything which is not the involuntary result of fleeting emotion, but the creation of time and will, any marriage, happy or unhappy, is infinitely more interesting and significant than any romance, however passionate.
W.H. AUDEN

I believe that love cannot be bought except with love, and he who has a good wife wears heaven in his hat.

JOHN STEINBECK

The man who has an ugly wife, holds his reputation safe.

PORTUGUESE PROVERB

Marriage: a master, a mistress and two slaves, making in all, two.

AMBROSE BIERCE

Marriage may often be a stormy lake, but celibacy is almost always a muddy horse-pond.

THOMAS LOVE PEACOCK

If you are afraid of loneliness, don't marry.

ANTON CHEKHOV

I can nail my left palm
    to the left-hand cross-piece but
I can't do everything myself.
    I need a hand to nail the right,
a help, a love, a you, a wife.

ALAN DUGAN

The true index of a man's character is the health of his wife.

CYRIL CONNOLLY

We want playmates we can own.

JULES FEIFFER

Marriage is a great institution, but I'm not ready for an institution.

MAE WEST

I tended to place my wife under a pedestal.

WOODY ALLEN

The only really indecent people are the chaste.

J.K. HUYSMANS

Whom God has put asunder, why should man put together?

RALPH WALDO EMERSON

Nothing is so much to be shunned as sex relations.

SAINT AUGUSTINE

Love is an ideal thing, marriage a real thing; a confusion of the real and the ideal never goes unpunished.

JOHANN WOLFGANG GOETHE

Marriage is a desperate thing. The frogs in Aesop were extremely wise; they had a great mind to some water, but they would not leap into the well, because they could not get out again.

JOHN SELDON

It is a mistake for a taciturn, serious-minded woman to marry a jovial man, but not for a serious-minded man to marry a light-hearted woman.

JOHANN WOLFGANG GOETHE

The romantic prestige of adultery comes from exaggerating the importance of chastity in the unmarried. If fornication were no sin, then adultery would be condemned, for it is a token form of murder. We do not murder the rival husband or wife but we murder their image in the eyes of those whom they love and so prepare for the cancer of the ego and the slow death by desertion.

CYRIL CONNOLLY

Forty years of romance make a woman look like a ruin and forty years of marriage make her look like a public building.

OSCAR WILDE

A woman unsatisfied must have luxuries. But a woman who loves a man would sleep on a board.

D.H. LAWRENCE

The man who enters his wife's dressing room is either a philosopher or a fool.

HONORÉ DE BALZAC

For a man and female to live continuously together is, biologically speaking, an extremely unnatural condition.

ROBERT BRIFFAULT

So heavy is the chain of wedlock that it needs two to carry it, and sometimes three.

ALEXANDRE DUMAS

Marriage is the only adventure open to the cowardly.

VOLTAIRE

If you marry, you will regret it; if you don't marry, you will also regret it.

SØREN KIERKEGAARD

The complaints which anyone voices against his mate indicate exactly the qualities which stimulated attraction before marriage.

DR. RUDOLPH DREIKURS

Only the strong of heart can be well married, since they do not turn to marriage to supply what no other human being can ever get from another—a sure sense of the fortress within himself.

MAX LERNER

At noon I home to dinner with my poor wife, with whom now-a-days I enjoy great pleasure in her company and learning of Arithmetic.

SAMUEL PEPYS

Even the God of Calvin never judged anyone as harshly as married couples judge each other.

WILFRID SHEED

The music at a wedding procession always reminds me of the music of soldiers going into battle.

HEINRICH HEINE

Husbands are like fires—they go out when unattended.

ZSA ZSA GABOR

No matter how happily a woman may be married, it always pleases her to discover that there is a nice man who wishes that she were not.

H.L. MENCKEN

In literature as in love, we are astonished at what is chosen by others.

ANDRÉ MAUROIS

If you meddle in other people's marriages you may lose a friend, but acquire his wife.

EDWARD DAHLBERG

The institution of marriage is just formalizing an emotion, an attempt to make it seem permanent. The emotion will last or it won't last; nothing can guarantee it. But as society becomes more and more unstable, as traditions break up, there will have to be a small unit of faithfulness, at least one person upon whom another person can depend, or society may disintegrate into madness.

JOYCE CAROL OATES

May I wish for you the knowledge (I'm getting a little heavy-handed here) that Marriages do not Take Place, they are made by hand; that there is always an element of discipline involved; that however perfect the honeymoon, the time will come, however brief it is, when you will wish she would fall downstairs and break a leg. That goes for her too. But the mood will pass, if you give it time.

RAYMOND CHANDLER

It seems that marriage is not one of my talents. I've been much happier unmarried than married. I'm probably unmarriageable now. I just can't imagine a marriage that would make sense to me. Once you've passed thirty, I think, it becomes harder and harder for a woman to do. It's easy when you're a teenager; perhaps that's the built-in mechanism for continuation of the species.

DORIS LESSING

The most tragic breakings-up are of those couples who have married young and who have enjoyed seven years of happiness, after which the banked fires of passion and independence explode—and without knowing why, for they still love each other, they set about accomplishing their common destruction.

CYRIL CONNOLLY

Everyone, naturally, wants love, but the real thing, when it arrives, is cruel, disconcerting, and frightening. One's partner refuses merely to be an object, a thing, an impersonal presence, and demands one's precious time, careful reflection, and emotional entanglement.

MICHAEL NOVAL

A lady's imagination is very rapid; it jumps from admiration to love, from love to matrimony, in a moment.

JANE AUSTEN

Adultery is extravagance.

MAXINE HONG KINGSTON

It destroys one's nerves to be amiable every day to the same human being.

BENJAMIN DISRAELI

When there's marriage without love, there will be love without marriage.

BENJAMIN FRANKLIN

All things in life are a mingling of bitterness and joy; war has its delights, and marriage its alarms.

LA FONTAINE

A happy marriage is a long conversation which always seems too short.

ANDRÉ MAUROIS

There are four stages to a marriage. First there's the affair, then the marriage, then children and finally the fourth stage, without which you cannot know a woman, the divorce.

NORMAN MAILER

The value of marriage is not that adults produce children, but that children produce adults.

PETER DE VRIES

It is just as hard to live with the person we love as to love the person we live with.

JEAN ROSTAND

It is easier to live through someone else than to become complete yourself.

BETTY FRIEDAN

There are women whose infidelities are the only link they still have with their husbands.

SACHA GUITRY

I would rather go to bed with Lillian Russell stark naked than Ulysses S. Grant in full military regalia.

MARK TWAIN

The best part of married life is the fights—the rest is merely so-so.

THORNTON WILDER

It doesn't matter what you do in the bedroom as long as you don't do it in the street and frighten the horses.

MRS. PATRICK CAMPBELL

Marriage is hardly a thing that one can do now and then—except in America.

OSCAR WILDE

If married couples did not live together, happy marriages would be more frequent.

FRIEDRICH NIETZSCHE

An archaeologist is the best husband any woman can have—the older she gets the more he is interested in her.

AGATHA CHRISTIE

A woman should never use her husband as her confessor; it demands more virtue of him than his situation allows.

GEORGE SAND

In a husband, there is only a man; in a married woman there is a man, a father, a mother, and a woman.

HONORÉ DE BALZAC

Variability is one of the virtues of a woman. It obviates the crude requirements of polygamy. If you have one good wife, you are sure to have a spiritual harem.

G.K. CHESTERTON

I have learned that only two things are necessary to keep one's wife happy. First, let her think she's having her way. And second, let her have it.

LYNDON BAINES JOHNSON

A man has no business to marry a woman who can't make him miserable. It means she can't make him happy.

ANONYMOUS

By all means marry; if you get a good wife, you'll become happy; if you get a bad one, you'll become a philosopher.

SOCRATES

There are only about twenty murders a year in London and not all are serious—some are just husbands killing their wives.

POLICE COMMANDER G.H. HATHERILL

The worst reconciliation is better than the best divorce.
CERVANTES

Marriage is the aftermath of love.
NOEL COWARD

She who would long retain her power must use her lover ill.
OVID

Love makes itself felt not in the desire for copulation (a desire that extends to an infinite number of women) but in the desire for a shared sleep (a desire limited to one woman).
MILAN KUNDERA

Sin is not hurtful because it is forbidden, but it is forbidden because it is hurtful.
BENJAMIN FRANKLIN

Perhaps that is what love is—the momentary or prolonged refusal to think of another person in terms of power.
PHYLLIS ROSE

There are encounters, there are feelings, when everything is given at once and a continuation is not necessary. To continue is, after all, to put to the test.
MARINA TSVETAEVA

Most of us love from our need to love not because we find someone deserving.
NIKKI GIOVANNI

The violence of love is as much to be dreaded as that of hate.

HENRY DAVID THOREAU

As is usual with most lovers in the city, they were troubled by the lack of that essential need of love—a meeting place.

THOMAS WOLFE

The heart of another is a dark forest, always, no matter how close it has been to one's own.

WILLA CATHER

One of the difficulties that a man has to cope with as he goes through life is what to do about the persons with whom he has once been intimate and whose interest for him has in due course subsided.

W. SOMERSET MAUGHAM

Passion will obscure our sense so that we eat sad stuff and call it nectar.

W.C. WILLIAMS

To be a lover is not to make love, but to find a new way to live.

PAUL LA COUR

To put it simply, one is changed by what one loves, sometimes to the point of losing one's entire identity.

JOSEPH BRODSKY

At the beginning of love and at its end the lovers are embarrassed to be left alone.

LA BRUYÈRE

A lover without discretion is no lover at all.

THOMAS HARDY

Oh hasten not this loving act,
Rapture where self and not-self meet:
My life has been the awaiting you,
Your footfall was my own heart's beat.

PAUL VALÉRY

Return often and take me at night
When the lips and the skin remember. . .

C.P. CAVAFY

My Oberon! What visions I have seen!
Me thought I was enamoured of an ass.

WILLIAM SHAKESPEARE

Faithfulness is one of the marks of genius.

CHARLES BAUDELAIRE

If we love we must not live as other men and women do—I cannot brook the wolfsbane of fashion and foppery and tattle. You must be mine to die upon the rack if I want you . . . Good bye! I kiss you—O the torments!

JOHN KEATS (letter to Fanny Brawne)

Can a man take fire in his bosom,
  and his clothes not be burned?
Can one go upon hot coals, and his feet
  not be burned?
  PROVERBS

A sneeze absorbs all the functions of the soul as much as the
sexual act.
  BLAISE PASCAL

Passion is the element in which we live; without it, we
hardly vegetate.
  LORD BYRON

Jealousy would be far less tortuous if we understood that
love is a passion entirely unrelated to our merits.
  PAUL ELDRIDGE

I wish there was something between love and friendship
that I could tender him; and some gesture, not quite a
caress, I could give him. A sort of smoothing.
  LOUISE BOGAN

Many a man has fallen in love with a girl in a light so dim
he would not have chosen a suit by it.
  MAURICE CHEVALIER

I wonder, by my troth, what you and I
Did, till we lov'd?
  JOHN DONNE

The desire for desires: boredom.
LEO TOLSTOI

Love is the only effective counter to death.
MAUREEN DUFFY

There must be the copulating and generating force of love behind every effort destined to be successful.
HENRY DAVID THOREAU

Complete physical union between two people is the rarest sensation which life can provide—and yet not quite real, for it stops when the telephone rings. Such a passion can be maintained at full strength only by the admixture of more unhappiness (jealousy, rows, renunciation) or more and more artificiality (alcohol and other technical illusions). Who escapes this heaven may never have lived, who exists for it alone is soon extinguished.
CYRIL CONNOLLY

Had we but world enough and time,
This coyness, Lady, were no crime.
We would sit down, and think which way
To walk, and pass our long love's day.
ANDREW MARVELL

The human face in love, which Ovid said was made to reflect the stars, see how its expression is only one of mad ferocity or death-like surrender.
CHARLES BAUDELAIRE

Fain would I kiss my Julia's dainty Leg,
Which is as white and hair-less as an egge.
ROBERT HERRICK

It is easier to keep half a dozen lovers guessing than to keep
one lover after he has stopped guessing.
HELEN ROWLAND

Love letters should always be dictated to a secretary.
ANONYMOUS

You don't know how convincing your love letters are until
your wife intercepts them.
ANONYMOUS

I want to do with you
What spring does
With the cherry trees.
PABLO NERUDA

Our two lives:
  Between them is the life
    Of the cherry flowers.
BASHŌ

The quarrelling of lovers is the renewal of love.
TERENCE

Skill makes love unending.
OVID

The heart may think it knows better; the sense knows that absence blots people out.
ELIZABETH BOWEN

It is overdoing the thing to die of love.
FRENCH PROVERB

Evil is to love what mystery is to intelligence.
SIMONE WEIL

Let every lover be pale; that is the color that suits him.
OVID

Herodotus tells us that in cold countries beasts very seldom have horns, but in hot they have very large ones. This might bear a pleasant application.
JONATHAN SWIFT

What men call gallantry, and gods adultery,
Is much more common where the climate's sultry.
LORD BYRON

More than half your friend is lost to you when he falls in love.
MME. DE SARTORY

A man does not look behind the door unless he has stood there himself.
HENRI DU BOIS

Love, like death, is congenial to a novelist because it ends a book conveniently. He can make it a permanency, and his readers easily acquiesce, because one of the illusions attached to love is that it will be permanent. Not has been—will be.

E.M. FORSTER

For a Horse of youth, strength and lustinesse, eight Mares are a full number.

JERVIS MARKHAM

As a jealous man, I suffer four times over: because I am jealous, because I blame myself for being so, because I fear that my jealousy will wound the other, because I allow myself to be subject to a banality: I suffer from being excluded, from being aggressive, from being crazy, and from being common.

ROLAND BARTHES

. . . For when I glance at you even an instant, I can no longer utter a word: my tongue thickens to a lump, and beneath my skin breaks out a subtle fire: my eyes are blind, my ears filled with humming, and sweat streams down my body, I am seized by a sudden shuddering; I turn greener than grass, and in a moment more, I feel I shall die.

SAPPHO

The only sin passion can commit is to be joyless.

DOROTHY SAYERS

To write a good love letter, you ought to begin without knowing what you mean to say, and to finish without knowing what you have written.

JEAN JACQUES ROUSSEAU

The poet . . . like the lover . . . is a person unable to reconcile what he knows with what he feels. His peculiarity is that he is under a certain compulsion to do so.

BABETTE DEUTSCH

Words are only painted fire; a look is the fire itself.

MARK TWAIN

The clever man, the clever man
How wisely did he reason!
But now, alack, his wits are gone,
His wisdom's out of season.

The glances of a maiden's eye
Have turned his head to jelly;
A monkey tumbled from a tree
Could not look half so silly!

THOMAS MANN

To Debbie Pookie Poople Pips from Petey Popsy Pooples—I love you—be mine.

THE TIMES OF LONDON, *Valentine Message*

To abuse a man is a lover-like thing and gives him rights.

JOYCE CAREY

The average man is more interested in a woman who is interested in him than he is in a woman with beautiful legs.

MARLENE DIETRICH

I wasn't kissing her, I was whispering in her mouth.

CHICO MARX

Life's short and we never have enough time for the hearts of those who travel the way with us. O, be swift to love! Make haste to be kind.

HENRI-FRÉDÉRICK AMIEL

I like young girls. Their stories are shorter.

THOMAS MCGUANE

For flavor, instant sex will never supersede the stuff you have to peel and cook.

QUENTIN CRISP

Quarrels in France strengthen a love affair. In America they end it.

NED ROREM

Power is the great aphrodisiac.

HENRY KISSINGER

If it is not erotic, it is not interesting.

FERNANDO ARRABAL

Truth is a great flirt.

FRANZ LISZT

It must be admitted that we English have sex on the brain, which is a very unfortunate place to have it.
MALCOLM MUGGERIDGE

I made no advances to her, but she accepted them.
LOUIS SCUTENAIRE

We are not the same persons this year as last; nor are those we love. It is a happy chance if we, changing, continue to love a changed person.
W. SOMERSET MAUGHAM

Fashions in sin change.
LILLIAN HELLMAN

When two men fight over a woman, it's the fight they want, not the woman.
BRENDAN FRANCIS

If you would understand men, study women.
FRENCH PROVERB

A wise woman never yields by appointment.
STENDHAL

Men are those creatures with two legs and eight hands.
JAYNE MANSFIELD

Women's being is an existence for something else.
SØREN KIERKEGAARD

A woman's ornament is her hair.
SAINT PAUL

Man makes love by braggadocio, and woman makes love by listening.
H.L. MENCKEN

It is probable that both in life and in art the values of a woman are not the values of a man.
VIRGINIA WOOLF

A woman's nobility was contained in woman's mystery. That is the secret strength of the eternal feminine: suggestion.
ISAK DINESEN

I've never been able to work without a woman to love. Perhaps I'm cruel. They are earth and sky and warmth and light to me. I'm like an Irish peasant, taking potatoes out of the ground. I live by the woman loved. I take from her. I know damned well I don't give enough.
SHERWOOD ANDERSON

I must raise myself to a higher level in order to rouse new impulses in her.
VINCENT VAN GOGH

No woman should allow herself to be possessed by any male but the devil.
ISAK DINESEN

An intelligent woman is a woman with whom one can be as stupid as one wants.

PAUL VALÉRY

The thing that is repugnant and monstrous about the prostitute is her contradiction of feminine nature, by virtue of which she offers the anonymous man, the public, that hidden personality which ought to be revealed only to the chosen one. To such a degree is this a negation of feminine character, that a scrupulous man feels an instinctive aversion toward the prostitute, as if, in spite of her female body, there were a masculine spirit in her.

ORTEGA Y GASSET

I have never loved anyone for love's sake, except, perhaps, Josephine—a little.

NAPOLEON I

The more women look in the mirror the less they look to their house.

FRENCH PROVERB

It takes all sorts to make a sex.

SAKI

Men are the cause of women hating one another.

LA BRUYÉRE

Women like silent men. They think they're listening.

MARCEL ACHARD

We are uneasy with an affectionate man, for we are positive he wants something of us, particularly our love.

EDWARD DAHLBERG

Men would be saints if they loved heaven as well as they do women.

SAINT THOMAS

It is useless to watch a bad woman.

SPANISH PROVERB

I had a sister much older than myself, from whose modesty and goodness, which were great, I learned nothing.

SAINT TERESA

When it comes to women, modern men are idiots. They don't know what they want, and so they never want, permanently, what they get. They want a cream cake that is at the same time ham and eggs and at the same time porridge. They are fools. If only women weren't bound by fate to play up to them.

D.H. LAWRENCE

One inevitable consequence of falling deeply in love is the realization that no one has yet adequately described the torment and ecstasy of your condition—and the knowledge that you will try and fail to do so.

WILLIAM JAY SMITH

The woman who loves both, deserves both.
PORTUGUESE PROVERB

It's quite right what they say: the three most beautiful sights in the world are a ship in full sail, a galloping horse, and a woman dancing.
HONORÉ DE BALZAC

A man can deceive his fiancée or his mistress as much as he likes, and, in the eyes of a woman he loves, an ass may pass for a philosopher; but a daughter is a different matter.
ANTON CHEKHOV

When a woman is awakened, when she gets the man she wants, she is amazing, amazing . . . sensuality is a whole separate world. Love is like a mine. You go deeper and deeper. There are passages, caves, whole strata. You discover entire geological eras.
CHRISTOPHER ISHERWOOD

From the first to the last Katherine appeared to me a totally exquisite being. Everything she did or said had its own manifest validity. I do not think it ever entered my head, at any time, to criticize her in any way. And certainly for a long while I was secretly astonished that she should have chosen me.
JOHN MIDDLETON MURRAY (*about Katherine Mansfield*)

Body of my woman, I will live on through your
marvelousness.
My thirst, my desire without end, my wavering road!
Dark river beds down which the eternal thirst is flowing,
and the fatigue is flowing, and the grief without shore.
    PABLO NERUDA

I hardly know you, and already I say to myself:
Will she never understand how her person exalts
all that there is in me of blood and fire?
    CARLOS PELLICER

No woman ever hates a man for being in love with her; but
many a woman hates a man for being her friend.
    ALEXANDER POPE

The less one loves a woman, the surer one is of possessing
her.
    ALEXANDER PUSHKIN

When every unkind word about women has been said, we
have still to admit, with Byron, that they are nicer than
men. They are more devoted, more unselfish, and more
emotionally sincere. When the long fuse of cruelty, deceit
and revenge is set alight, it is male thoughtlessness which
has fired it.
    CYRIL CONNOLLY

A woman and a hen are soon lost by gadding about.
    SPANISH PROVERB

The fickleness of the woman I love is only equaled by the infernal constancy of the women who love me.

BERNARD SHAW

There is one woman whom fate has destined for each of us. If we miss her, we are saved.

ANONYMOUS

For a time men will endure scenes of anger and jealousy from the women they deeply love. Some prefer agitated love affairs as they prefer rough seas to calm ones; but most of them are definitely peace-loving. They are easily won by good temper, simplicity and gentleness, especially if some mad woman has previously cured them of their taste for violence.

ANDRÉ MAUROIS

Women love men for their defects; if men have enough of them, women will forgive them everything, even their gigantic intellects.

OSCAR WILDE

A gentleman is a patient wolf.

HENRIETTA TIARKS

Alas! coquettes are but too rare. 'Tis a career that requires great abilities, infinite pains, a gay and airy spirit. 'Tis the coquette that provides all amusement . . . She is the soul of the house, the salt of the banquet.

BENJAMIN DISRAELI

A man may be said to love most truly that woman in whose company he can feel drowsy in comfort.

GEORGE JEAN NATHAN

The more serious the face, the more beautiful the smile.

CHATEAUBRIAND

A man has missed something if he has never woken up in an anonymous bed beside a face he'll never see again, and if he has never left a brothel at dawn feeling like jumping off a bridge into the river out of sheer physical disgust with life.

GUSTAVE FLAUBERT

A man is already halfway in love with any woman who listens to him.

BRENDAN FRANCIS

I love Mickey Mouse more than any woman I've ever known.

WALT DISNEY

Heaven has no rage like love to hatred turned,
Nor Hell a fury like a woman scorned.

WILLIAM CONGREVE

In all your amours you should prefer old women to young ones . . . they have greater knowledge of the world.

BENJAMIN FRANKLIN

Why are women so much more interesting to men than
men are to women?

VIRGINIA WOOLF

The only way a woman can ever reform a man is by boring
him so completely that he loses all possible interest in life.

OSCAR WILDE

A man defending husbands vs. wives or men vs. women has
got about as much chance as a traffic policeman trying to
stop a mad dog by blowing two whistles.

RING LARDNER

When women kiss it always reminds one of prize fighters
shaking hands.

H.L. MENCKEN

Prudery is a form of avarice.

STENDHAL

It is best to have a face which neither dazzles nor frightens,
and with mine I get on well with friends of both sexes.

GEORGE SAND

When choosing between two evils I always like to take the
one I've never tried before.

MAE WEST

A maid that laughs is half taken.

ENGLISH PROVERB

If a woman hasn't got a tiny streak of the harlot in her, she's a dry stick.

D.H. LAWRENCE

Women over thirty are at their best, but men over thirty are too old to recognize it.

JEAN-PAUL BELMONDO

He wondered why sexual shyness, which excites the desire of dissolute women, arouses the contempt of decent ones.

COLETTE

Woman is the most superstitious animal beneath the moon. When a woman has a premonition that Tuesday will be a disaster, to which a man pays no heed, he will very likely lose his fortune then. This is not meant to be an occult or mystic remark. The female body is a vessel, and the universe drops its secrets into her far more quickly than it communicates them to the male.

EDWARD DAHLBERG

As I grow older and older
And totter toward the tomb
I find I care less and less
Who goes to bed with whom.

DOROTHY SAYERS